De Chirico's Threads

for Yura

Carol Rumens
De Chirico's Threads

SEREN

Seren is the book imprint of
Poetry Wales Press Ltd.
57 Nolton Street, Bridgend, Wales, CF31 3AE
www.serenbooks.com

ISBN: 978-1-85411-534-8

A CIP record for this title is available from the British Library.

The publisher acknowledges the financial assistance of the Welsh Books Council.

Cover art: Giorgio De Chirico (1888-1978): 'The Duo' (Les mannequins de la Tour
Rose), 1915. New York, Museum of Modern Art (MoMA). Oil on canvas, 81.9 x 59
cm. James Thrall Soby Bequest. Acc. n.: 1213.1979.
© 2010. Digital image, The Museum of Modern Art, New York/Scala, Florence

Printed in Bembo by Bell & Bain Ltd., Glasgow.

Author's website/blog: www.carolrumens.co.uk

Contents

Part One: Ice and Fire:

Sonnets for Late-Elizabethan Lovers

1. The Birth of Venus

"I can tell from here... what the inhabitants of Venus are like; they resemble the Moors of Granada; a small black people, burned by the sun, full of wit and fire, always in love, writing verse, fond of music, arranging festivals, dances, and tournaments every day." – Bernard de Fontenelle, 1686.

Bernard de Fontenelle, you took a shine
To Venus, but we've learned a thing or two
Since then. She's mostly cracked volcanic plain,
Her clouds are sulphur (pray they never rain)
And though the Hubble's filter bathes her blue,
Her oceans warmed and went. Oh, world of dew!

She warns us: cool it. Yet, as your eyes wished her
Life, so we construct her centre-fold
Of continents into the foamy world
Of Terra Aphrodite, Terra Ishtar,
As if such radiance figured potency –
Love-comet Zeus not taking no, the shroud·
Slick with glycine. Sea or no sea,
Boats burn for Venus still. And gods are formed from cloud.

2. Alba

It was this morning's REM sleep, and the dream
Began in Kwiksell, or was it Costsaver?
I was near the check-out when, from another room,
He beckoned, held out a gift: *lactuca sativa*!
It was my boss. I was pale and dumb as a foetus,
And filmed with milky saliva
As I stretched my hand to the globe of his home-grown lettuce.

Though I stalked him all day in the annex of Human Resources,
He had far too much on his plate
To observe the green gleam of my glances.
Oh, let me dream more and lie late,
Till our fingers melt through the lattice
Of leaves, and he beckons me onto his office-lounger,
And offers my lips his salad-bowl, *prêt-à-manger*.

3. The Soldier's Girl-Friend

Call-up. And it's as if I'd never met him
And wouldn't want to. Others wave goodbye.
I'm hanky-less and dry.
My simple transitives? Dump him or regret him.

I dreamed I found his tent on the front-line.
His face was stitched. His penis would have failed
The *pleased-to-see-me* test. He hasn't emailed…
His war has no intelligence of mine.

I google LOVE POEMS, savour crushed desire:
Our courtship, whose whole concept's mediaeval,
Shivers between Petrarch's ice and fire.

Girls with *intelligence of love*, compare
His tropes with what the literal-minded bomber:
Does with the pearls and rubies a young man's summer.

4. De Chirico Paints Ariadne on Naxos

In a household that hid death from childhood,
a boy is handed the dream-death of his sister.
A sheet, dragged through a railing. Harsh sobbing engines.
He climbs in again and again to rescue her.

You can't marry sisters, stupid. You can't unpeel the dead
from their dirty sheets, their wrap of liquefied stone.
But there is another: *puella vagula*, vague pupa.
Ariadne smiles. You un-tangle a little thread.

> *"And now the sun has come to a high halt*
> *In the middle of the sky.*
> *And the statue in eternal happiness*
> *Immerses her soul in contemplating the shadow."*

You pray in the Casa d'Arte. You have sinned. You know who it is
you've left behind on Naxos. Art is brief. Life longer is.

(Note: italicised lines are from a fragment of poetry by Giorgio de Chirico)

5. Lines

I've read his poems: a double-dim perception,
Long shots through pin-holes. Guess I really found
Only myself – that old romantic friend,
Myself – and 'long withdrawing' self-deception

I closed the programme. Me. The mouse ran down
And sideways over a diminished future:
Laura could have embroidered quite a figure
For love's new life, dead to the world, online.

We meet sometimes. That's stranger. How to play
With little offices and light routines
At war with time? It isn't love to say

I love him, though I prove the permanent way
Between us on interminable returns
That end in Lent and never Lady Day.

6. Canzone for an Envelope

If we'd ever conversed not as client and consulente
But comrades: if I'd known how to employ my employer
That night we discussed the best way to cook penne al dente
And the delegates started to dance in the aisles of La Gioia:

If our meetings had ended on time and your sense of occasion
Had tended to lunch… or, supposing I hadn't been frightened
(Disguising myself as far-sighted) to issue my own invitation
Gracious-flirtatiously: had I not felt so enlightened,

Telling myself 'There's no hope, you're a dope, don't pretend it.
La freccia non funczione' – this phoney canzone
By now would have charmed you, and here I would happily end it.

But since, without reason or future or shame, I've not burned it,
It's sealed, with two licks and a tear. Never read it, or only
After I'm gone, *per favore, Signor. Draw your own conclusione.*

7. Theatres

Wed to his roadside slut, my husband came
Home in that awful suit-case. Massive-shouldered,
He walked on smaller shoulders
Until he slipped and darkened. I became

A tower of speaking flame, a lilied angel,
Who blushed and looked translucent without help
From Make-up. Tears made little pearls. That helped.
I saw myself divine from every angle,

And all the media trusting me to play
My part, the starry part a young girl's owed,
If she's a woman widowed,

her leading man all crammed with lead. Some play!
I court the camera's I.E.D. like he
crawled to that bitch. Theatre's in our blood.

8. The White Stag

It was the bitter season, early spring.
At sunrise, on some laurel-shaded grass,
Islanded where the two rivers pass,
A white stag, golden-horned, stood quivering.

Charmed by his glances, I dropped everything
And hurried after him. Bankers amass
Their wealth by being similarly ruthless,
The tough work eased by money's pleasant ring.

Closing in, as his handsome throat turned,
I saw inscribed in diamonds and warm topaz:
'Don't touch! This deer belongs to Caesar's herd.'

It was already noon, the sun had burned
Westward; still I couldn't rest my eyes
Till water drowned them, and he disappeared.

'The White Stag' is a re-working of Petrarch's
'Una Candida Cerva' (*Rime* 190).

Part Two:
Itinerary Through a Photograph Album

Count Dracula Creates his Online Profile

He had several ideas of himself, or himselves.
His Baroque image, with powdered plaits and the sultry
crimson wash of his train, was a difficult one.
Filmic, he thought, but too much.

He could swish a cape, or doff a silk topper, his sweeping off-er, his tile,
with sheer *aristo* style for a wow-them bow:
He could do Oscar Wilde in an oyster wasp-waister, the pearls
dripping like love-sick tears. Not him.

There were teen-spirit vampires in trainers, handsome off-spring
he didn't love, but apparently his, and the latest
craze. They shlepped around Starbucks, sipped synthetic blood
through a twisty straw. Pathetic, though girls adored them.

Not him. He'd been an old wolf, he'd snarled and pawed and slurped.
He was still a bit of an animal, and why not?
But beauties didn't want real beasts any longer.
He played clip after clip: not one was his true profile.

He decided to be himself, fess up to his years (six hundred),
the snoring, the holes in his memory. But there was no face in the glass
to speak of. And, if he made it up, how could he make it stick?
He'd never kept a look. His face fell apart

at the least provocation. Shape-shifter? Shaman? Actor?
Hardly the type for a middle-aged English Rose!
He remembered Mina's gasp when he'd introduced himself.
'A prince, no less!' Bloody class-ridden Brits. He practised his Eton smirk

as his rat-feet fingers found the words: 'A genuine Count...'

On the Autistic Spectrum

You were always a disaster;
Plaits and laces hung awry.
You rode, you riled, school's roller-coaster;
Bright, they said, but doesn't try:
   You hated words like *try*.

Nurture ruled us then, not nature,
So you blamed a style of care
Where each day was saved for later
Till your house ran out of air,
   But gave itself an 'air.'

Mother wanted other babies;
You were not her baby bright.
Soon she'd classed you with the crazies.
Mummy knew. You weren't quite right
   And you'd go west, all right.

Failure, here's your diagnosis:
You're too old for your disease.
Treasure it. There's no prognosis
But the word. It's a release
   Of sorts, a coiled release.

Artist-autist, timid, gallant,
Still beginning at the end,
It was useless to have talent
If you couldn't make a friend
   And didn't need a friend.

They won't know the face and body
When they find you on the floor.
Some believe you've died already
Though you're smiling more and more
   And more and more and more.

The Solitary Bride

The street is familiar in the usual way, but the light today strikes from it flashes of more distant memory. It's like the moment you suspect water, a thread of river or sea just becoming visible from a train widow, destabilising the horizon. Is it only the sky? No, it's not only the sky.

Once, when the September shadows were like this, big and dark compared with the bright white buildings, when the plane trees' small foliage was so green it was almost navy-blue, I walked down this street as a believer might walk through a temple courtyard. I was going home, it was lunch-time: I was stealing a couple of hours from work.

It wasn't the first time. I was, as people still sometimes say without irony, 'in love.' He visited only occasionally: I was a minor part of his routine, fitted in with difficulty. You could say he didn't have a lot of time for me. It hardly mattered. What mattered to me then was that the intensities of my imagination could be expressed and shared, bodily.

This is what I mean by 'I was in love.'

And so I walked down the street, crowded then as now with medical students and Bloomsbury tourists and miscellaneous truth-seekers and bus-stop settlements, like a believer through a deserted temple courtyard. No, like a bride.

A bride in all her loneliness, her mind reduced to the shifting space between her bare skin and the inside of her dress, whose top layer is white or saffron or emerald. A bride in chinos and a sleeveless shirt, walking through an empty bright white courtyard, struck through with dense rectangles of shade. There were no wedding-guests. There was no priest, rustling in the temple.

We wouldn't have long together, maybe not even an hour. Perhaps we never made love again. This isn't a sad story. There were others. I always had enough desire for us both. It doesn't matter. It doesn't touch the white buildings and their shadows.

I walk down the darkly flashing street. There are no witnesses. I walk towards a hot, wide attic room with a geranium on the window-sill and a ridiculously small bed with a blue throw: I walk, quicker now, to the embrace that's reflected in the mirror over the gas-fire: to the necessarily quick undressing: to his perfectly fulfilling penis: to the way he looks at me – the look which always names me.

The train has moved or turned. The length of clear water-light is revealed.

The shadow of the bride moves over the pavement, moves inside me.

Naming, being named. This is all I mean by love.

Off the Hook

For Isabella

In those complicated days, only the rich
Had 'phones. The rest of us queued
To get into a tall red box: its windows were sticky
And it smelt of damp concrete and cigarette-smoke.
The telephone didn't look friendly,
Shiny-black on its ledge, a bakelite toad.

You'd pick the hand-set up, and hate the purr,
That rumble of hunger unappeasable.
You counted out heavy pennies, pushed Button A.
Fingered the wheel around and let it re-roll
- Three letters, four numbers. You wanted to run
When the paired rings resounded. How hopeless you were!

You stabbed Button B, and thought you might die.
The money clanked through loudly:
Your voice came out super-polite, as it did in 'Phone Land,
Leaving your mind quite dead behind one ear,
Telling him you couldn't come to the party,
You had too much homework. A complete lie.

Some live with their mobiles snug to their lips,
Or melting against their cheeks.
They belong to a different race. They sound so happy.
I bury mine, and panic at its warble.
And only in deepest love would I make a call
And not be relieved when I heard the 'engaged' beeps.

But when it's your voice, Isabella, saying hello,
So brave and clear, with nothing at all phoney
(Ahem) in your yes and no, I see why it's good
To talk. I wish you a lifetime of easy phoning.
Be mobile-merry, and never mind the bills
Or curse the bells. I'll stick to e-mail, though.

Diphthongs

In labour you grow old
you listen to the pain   you give it room
    to stretch a little wider and a little
                            wider till it tears a noise from you
that's not the child unless
                        the child is pain

You're interested at first   surprised to learn
    nature has set no limits
    your body   though you love it   sets no limits
        but tricks you with a little
        easy pain that's the beginning of
                    a wave that won't stop gathering when you say
                                                enough
                            fold back   give over

pain doesn't hesitate because a forehead
            shines or breath is
            harsh. Pain has its say   it burns
    enormous holes through prayers. *Pain will learn you.*

There are such diphthongs in the word   pain
                    you're opening like the future
                                    and all it says is death
and death's like this
                    perhaps
                            or dying is

But this
    time it's not death. Remember
the other meaning   breathe it   rhyme it further
            and harder   wider   harder   till wide nature
        is satisfied   closes her golden eye
                relents. Your turn.
                        You turn

you turn towards
    the little wounded human face   the only
      the only vowel   and shining
                  there's no limit to your shining

The Wobble

There are some minds happiest among archives.
We track their progress through the world of crude,
Their quick adjustments, their refined evasions,
When offered to the battlefields where treason
Itself may not be strategy enough.
We watch with shy concern, the way you watch
A small child standing on a swivel-chair.
You grip the seat, she flies above the keyboard,
Chagall-like. From her hands, the star-tailed data
Evolve and swim. To such an art of balance –
To such an art – the wobble's integral.
There are some minds so happy among archives
They dance there sometimes, witty as their toes.

Imaginary Painting by De Chirico:
the Birth of the Poet

I was pinned to the top of my street,
wrapped in a wind that was wrapping me in leaves.
When it abated I shook my heavy, rustling
self towards home, the home a human would
require, half tree in a street no longer street.

Where houses used to stand (mine, too!) there lay
the pools and caverns and hills of a building site,
vast, with a sunset rust and blue above it.
I peered through the slats of the fencing. Something wept
at my back: "They're turning it into a bloody fairground!

Where will we live?"
                           "In the drain," I suggested rudely.
This was no longer my street and I was quondam.
        I pretended to bear   the burden
        I pretended to be   the burden
of branches like compound fractures, and the dusty taste of leaves
and no front door. The drain-man gurgled to nothing.

I thought about growing roots as the first carousel
of black-spotted orange horses
rose from the dust, and the music began to prance:
a minuet of twinkling, high-stepping hooflets
just for me in my forest of fruitless enchantment.

The Old Crystal Palace 'High Level' Station

Grass-families have been migrating here for years
to crowd the platform's crumpling brow, and recycle
sleepers and rails and the bright tin sign, Alight
Here for the Crystal Palace, to a humbler universe.

A tossed-away fag, my father said, ignoring
the sabotage theories, had brought the 'people's palace'
down like a bomb. There were craters and blackened echoes
and meadow-blues: then money. The floodlit stadium, roaring.

What's any palace, though, but a beautiful game,
running on give and resistance and crystallised moments
of solo soaring? The architect loves his blueprints
as the manager, his shifty team: both work with the flammable.

Too late for the show, I played on the toppled heads
of plaster-cast Rome and the last train puffed away
from the High Level Station. Still the original stair-case,
crinoline-wide, meets its high-five of colonnades,

but the only commuters are pigeons. They bustle and moan
and the station waits like a soldier in a skirt,
staring at no horizon, holding the fort
on the tip of his spear – a sweetmeat for an old woman

forever his pudding-faced queen. The 'hollow square'
dissolves, the bricks shimmer off to the latest theatres:
More men, we need more men! So the legionaries, lancespades,
                                                    hoplites,
"the long and the short and the tall" – flow through the timer

like sand, like flame through stockades, like ripples invisibly
                                                    spilling
out of the lake where a child chucked stones at nothing.
For the planters of iron, these customs are an old habit.
Preserve it – our track-record of stealing the world –

and shine up the redbrick and terracotta mirrors,
till they show us how empty the turreted booking-hall
where the young fans scrap and chant, ghost armies just out of school,
arriving on cheap day-returns with their straw-hatted girls

at the foot of the twentieth-century, running too fast
up the ever-steepening steps, *get a gander at them crystals*
and nick one, Bill, if we're lucky. They spin through the echoing portals.
Below them, grass breaks stones. Ozymandias forms out of dust.

The Concentration-Camp Poplars Remember their First Gardeners

Because they had to be slaves before they died,
their hands were used, their feet were used, their spines
were bent and used, their breath was pumped, pumped,
pumped till the valves failed, their sweat was forced
or tricked from them, like their last spoon or shoe.

The grass is too young to be a suspect:
the signposts and the freshly surfaced walkways
that whisper, *you weren't born*, weren't born. But we –
choice seedlings for a smoke-screen (uprooted
like them, half-dead, like them) – we let them spill us
among the rocks they'd cursed and brashed that day.
Some were no longer standing. Some could kneel.

Their fingers chilled us, but they pushed us down,
down, our roots found soil. We sucked the rain
which, when they'd left, fell thickly with their falling.
Then, one by one we raised our arms, confessing
the stolen jewels, their lives. We could not shed them.

They grow in us. We pray our aching branches
may ferry them to the leaf-tips of your blindness.

Hurbinek's Children

i.m. the Rememberer, Primo Levi

Hurbinek, no-one's left to help you repeat
Your word, the first you tried.
You were born in hell. None of us could translate,
Though we speak so much, such a word.

On your arm's small L, a tattoo,
Full-sized. In your dark eyes' O, the hoard
Of life, all wasted. Who
Had scratched the word on the void

Of your brain? One who was kind?
Was anyone kind? What a language you'd have had,
If you'd kept on trying to find

Your tongue, till the hell sprang through
Your vocal chords, Hurbinek, and you knew
There was a language everyone understood.

Note: in *The Truce: A Survivor's Journey from Auschwitz*, Primo Levi wrote of the three-year-old Auschwitz survivor known as Hurbinek: "He died in the first days of March 1945, free but not redeemed. Nothing remains of him: he bears witness through these words of mine."

Shaped Matter

Poem beginning with an idea from Rilke's 'An Holderlin'★

We're not allowed to stay, no, not among
The most familiar things…These things may change
Their terms with us, however, and our lightest
Shadow, farthest cast, disturb or mist them.
Returning home, we grope for sameness, checking
Hen-heartedly that nothing's shattered, stolen
Or stone: only the kids are disappointed!
But gradually we notice a faint bruising
Or minor lesion – bloody work of absence
As it keeps playing catch with bloodless things.
We're not supposed to linger – but we linger,
Settling our toys and penny fairings, till they're
Leaning towards our myth. They're beautiful
Once more, because they bore us. Lust for boredom
Is why we linger with the beautiful.

Consider, from all those, the one person
Whose looks, so deeply known, you'll never know.
That poignant face went by. What's left but shorthand?
A few strokes we call metonymy –
The bored perfection of our editorship.
So we start work on love, curtailing, pinching
Its edges to the semblance of a thing,
A charm against all absence – faultless sameness.
We stay, we linger, knowing love is nothing
But matter waiting to be changed and slowly
Lost. We think by touching less we keep it.

"Abiding, not even in what we know best/ is given us…"
                    –(Trans. David Constantine)

Riddle

you were the glowing inks a punch-drunk God
smeared for his pledge: the bow
he slung away, laughing.
                              Gold-medal sprinter,
you gave the slip to earth-sky frontiers: gently
you widened Dido's wound, knowing the skills
of the hospice as a sideline,
and lowered yourself to rumour – grubby gold:
we still forgave your teasing

until   our deeper looking   teased you back and tore

          fatally
                    your see-through silk   we traced your

          scar of   light's   slow   travel

          (slow!)   through thickset air

                              on a rain-drop's shell, you turned

          in a moment's fading, faded

     we handled you
                         phenomenon   knifed you open

     somewhereover   never-land   we dropped you

          un-done your eight-fold

          cloth   all   holed

               your ribboned skin
     all the more wonderful, we said.

And seemingly you magnify us still:
you stretch the water in our eyes; glance over
our domes and spires, un-mocking. You could still lean down,
    Iris, and have mercy on the world.

Daylight Spending

Atrophied days begin with too much light,
Cut teeth too soon, develop, and start dying
Too young. They leave us to negotiate
The road that steepens after clocks start lying

Perhaps, though, they were lying earlier?
We've put them back for synchronicity
With our sweet flaws: the legless sleeps, the dither,
The touching faith in electricity.

The Mudstone Rainbow

Lake Ogwen, February

I waded out into the lake,
Panning for scraps of pearly grit;
And here's my catch – a brown mosaic
Of mudstones that deny all light
If water fails to mediate.
Their dripping, rusty slivers leave
Henna'd fingers, a soaked sleeve,
But something bare and true to like.

The flat-topped mountain's scimitar
Presses the sky and turns it pale.
That curve, those melting bands, compose
A modest rainbow of the soil,
No flame of green in it, scant rose:
From frosty grass to distant shale
It shrugs at what the water does
With wobbled shadow, hints of star.

Temples, I think, will never shine
Out of this earth, though houses might.
It seems a scrap-yard of lost time
When splats of refuse cleverly leapt
As handles into hands, as blades
Into the blood. Those stone-age shades
Take aim. The unknown alphabets
Spell fear, the known lie readerless.

Back to the stones. I brought them home,
Designer Paleozoic slate!
Restful, dusty, now room-warm,
Most of their fire and ice played out,
They promise nothing rainbow-bright
But silently amalgamate
The mystery of the last sea-bed
To mountains formed inside the head.

2084

Paired wheels and PV panels, ponds and hives
and garden-fields (citron and silvery-green
samplers, all hand-stitched) declare our ground.
We're scripture-safe: for each estate, one screen
only, daily rationing of down-loads.
That ice-bar, frilling in the distant sound,
that flood, in motion inches from the cross-roads
where we abolished runways and re-wound
the windmills, will be measured and contained –
the government says so. And the world will sail
over the carbon peak: we'll be in free-fall
the whole sweet way to paradise regained.

It's slow, of course. The children want to burn
anything that burns. They say we stole
the magic brand, and scraped the sun's wheel
to light it, so shut up: it's their turn
to hit the gas, tank up, ignore the brakes,
as children should. *Just let us be children,*
they wail from blazing consoles. And we tell them,
or try to, what it was to drive that borrowed
chariot, rocketing, spiralling with its florid
machinery in a thunder of gold tyres
down, down the yellowing sky-waste. *Oh infelix
Phaethon, earth grew nothing, then, but fires.
We drove death into childhood, just being children.*

Dig

That asphalt strip, gritty raw pink which flanks
The central reservation's monorail
Became their last resort, its narrow strand
The only place where anxious human walking
Could happen, *in extremis*. Trivial flotsam
Laps at the drainage grids: strange coins of soil,
Some bat-like thing —a biker's rotted glove? -
Dust-heaps the forests shed for dearth of leafage
And a white tissue-ball with one torn wing
Beating, flittering in the wind. Why bother
Examining this evidence of pathos,
Scrunched shyly like a precious human secret?
Whether it's food or make-up, blood or shit,
Can't matter if there's no-one's name on it.

Itinerary Through a Photograph Album

Quickly we move on our chain of moving selves
Though the journey we always remember has taken years:
We stopped at the stations, got out, strolled up and down,
Learnt voices, prices, hand-shakes, fluently settled
Into the customs, unique, yet lords of the local.
These ports and streets we remember by name – our name,
Yet we never touched their ground, never left the moving vehicle

East Ending

For Becky and Roly, and for Wilton's Music Hall

Cable Street, Royal Mint Street, Tower Hill,
East Smithfield: history swims
Through names too big for it, old working names
Blitzed by re-development, black and still
As stone that holds small life-forms in suspension.
We hate and love this torpor of museums.

Hate it, mostly. There are stones less rare,
Readable narratives
Threading, sprawling like a London bus queue –
That crush of cultural idioms in one stare.
The scag-mag little factories, done up new,
Shift post-code in a street, get real, get lives.

Yes, *real lives*. Lilacs out of dead money –
The terrace's mild *amour*
Propre of vases, lamps, wives who salaam
On steps to shine that cockney dream of Sunny-
Side-of-the-Street, sure as the Sally Army
Bawled in the gin-shop, 'Don't have any more!'

History? It's the writing on the walls
Of pubs, a fish-bar called The Codfather;
The inn we don't go in, The Artful Dodger;
The DLR train tracks it, and it falls
With shit and feathers from the clattering bridge;
It's seven white skull-caps crossing at the zebra

Towards (we notice now) a mosque's small tower,
So easy in its nook,
It might have jostled longer than St Paul's
Among the old brass necks of palaces, power-
Mills and ships. Will someone list our malls
One day, finding some pleasure in a look

That thinks itself sheer function, and improve
The grade 2 concrete with new polymers?
What's the true art of architects? To make it
New, to stitch the shoe we ought to fit?
Let them re-invent the shadow-book –
Not Stilnovisti but New Formalists!

We turn the corner into Ensign Street
Where the best brothels were, and the best turns,
And, prettily distressed as Daisy Bell,
She begs our custom – Wilton's Music Hall.
Her fragile balcony's a work-in-progress.
Be careful! She's fresh-bathed and tremulous,

Her tits like pearly scandals and her ankles
Barley-sugar. To restore the old,
Make old just new enough not to disturb
The ghost of Champagne Charley and his girls
Back-stage. It's kitsch. So what? So's Shakespeare's Globe.
An audience works the glitz until it's gold.

Word-perfect, we belt out those choruses
Oh, don't have any more, Mrs Moore!
And fill the wormy hollows with our noise
Or you won't find your front door, Mrs Moore!
Our mobiles wink from gallery to pit,
To catch the past, show us ourselves in it.

Sunset for the Under Fives

At first, it seems merely surprising, aberrant:
Grandpa, sailing the sunset beyond his pipe-smoke,
Grandma in rolled-down stockings, wandering off to play
And losing her marbles somewhere – a laugh-less adult joke.
We get it slowly. It happens not only to quaint
Creased folk, born long before us, this curious jaunt,
And sunset is not what they see, but the hard earth's turning away.

The Tadpole Goddess

My Lethe, motionless between green thickets
Where flags prick up their rust-stained saffron ears,
You hear no splash of oars, no dust-up of lost souls
Except for dragon-flies a-spin, and tadpoles
That hang like little mud-bubbles, expecting
Their childhood gloom to lift, and life bounce up in them.
Your spirit's airless, Lethe; boot-top-deep,
You're less ditch than a mouthful of saliva
Drained by a dental tube. So why this leaning
To breathe into your film of suspect glitters,
And leave my slutty kiss? The final flutter on
Posterity? Perhaps a faster current
Washes the tubers, where my hair would tangle
And pass, and finally drag me to pure water.
I'd travel free of earth, rapid and weightless
And miles out of my depth, my shadow flinging
north and north, my coughed-up lungs your rattles
To play with till their fragments swam like tadpoles.
I'd find my cold Elysium, and to keep.

Must Have

If not the person –
Their stuff.
Diamonds.
Windchimes.
Paperweights.
Watches.
Freezer-ready soul-food.
Give us the ash.
We'll do the animation.

Conversation

Without hearing, I learned to listen to you.

I learned, without a body, to make love to you.

I heard you faintly, worded your snarls or smiles,
The smell of your mood.

Sometimes, I'd imagine my hand moving
Over the parts you couldn't bear me to touch –
As idly, lightly, as I touch these lines.

Poems are born with little sign of pressure
And could be removed or lost with even less.

I tell them to speak to me about you. Never
Were poems anything more – except at first
When I hoped there'd be a reader to believe them.

Without reading, I learned to listen to you.
Believed, without any body, what it was to be loved.

A Lecherous Professor

It was the 'sixties, no-one thought anything of it:
He was handsome and fifty, a 'brilliant' philosopher,
And no-one supposed it was not by mutual consent
He dated the best-looking girl in our first-year seminar.

She was cool, she had a detached, proud way with her.
All of us took it for granted they were an 'item'
And wouldn't have dreamt of protesting. But were we disturbed?
Of course. Envy had entered our innocent class-room.

We were, looking back, a strange year. All women, uncertain,
Rushing ourselves. I fancied myself as a bride
In the jeans and Woolworth's ring of a student wedding.
And the brightest scholar of all was a suicide —

For love. Of course, I'm not blaming the professor.
Girls' gardens hatch their own serpents — the mirror that needs
To be lovely in someone's eyes, the ephemeral baby
Crying *be quick*, all the shoving of our own greeds.

And the 'real world' — uh oh, the real world
Grabs girls like sweets, and hadn't they better know it.
Had they? Well, they will certainly know it in time.
A university needn't run courses on it.

Something old-fashioned called 'the life of the mind'
(Once thought to damage the ovaries of young women)
Should have been treasured for us by that handsome professor
By letting us wander where looks and lusts are forgotten.

The professor died praised and famous. When I read
His obituaries, printed small and far as my youth,
I knew I'd been half in love with him, too. He was witty
And gracious and terribly polite, as he discoursed on
                                philosophical truth.

Catching the Tide at Llanfairfechan

The moment the tide turned, nothing was obviously different
Until I realised I was hearing this
Distant, constant surge that could have been
Merely the A55 or the wind in the rushes,
But which, in its depths, had trapped a waterfall,
Stroking my goose-fleshed shoulders like a promise.

The sea was still as far. But I started to walk
The mile or so of mud and mussel-slag,
Sands rippled every which way, sunlit loops
And plaits of moisture, isles where gulls sat cushioned,
Until I reached the shallows: there I met it –
The tide's desire. As it pushed against my ankles

I watched how it moved the length of that great shoreline,
Sending out long, furled feelers, getting in fast
Wherever the sand-level dipped and an old route opened.
Almost playful, foam-scraps ran about
Like kids in a race, their progress ragged, eager.
And the turned tide sang its song, and beat at my shins.

I argued: water is water, the earth turns.
Though it feels so willed, so almost passionate
The sea is neither in land-love nor land-loathing.
But of course I thought about those human occasions
When the mere fact of a tide insists you travel
In pulse after pulse of hope, ever more certain,

And utterly wrong, and headed for reversal.
I forced myself to see how the tide would retreat,
Again to advance and retreat, that perpetuum mobile,
When only one story's required: that the boat, coming in,
Means joy and increase and nothing ever after
The happily-ever-after, no more process,

No proof that even love repeats, decays…
Then I put all dark philosophy to one side,
And waded out till I could lean on the water
And pour myself forwards, find that moment where
The sky, all over the sea, and the sea, half over the land,
Seemed more than my fair share, my height's depth more than ample.

Englynion, Bangor Pier, November

I walk across the pearl-grey Menai Strait.
Then I wait at the pier's end,
Watching the broad ripples fanned

By a boat, one sea-mew swimming.
Through dimming light, as I turn –
Snow-bright Snowdon, a thin moon.

A Winter Prayer

i.m. Mick Imlah

A berry, flirting on the crowded holly,
Or dropped at its dark foot, slightly crumpled,
But certain that the folded good inside it,
Though not the word for spring, is still a word
As bitter, bright and crystal-complex...Lammas,
The earthed berry promises, good morrow.

A Christmas Home-Coming

i.m. my parents, Wilfred and Marjorie Lumley, and for my 65th. birthday

December, 1947 or '8:
You take the little bowl of sparkly light
Carefully by the stem – and raise your glass
Of water-wine. A joke, then there's a kiss
You vaguely disapprove of. Daddy's home,
Not yet demobbed, but merry. So we'll leave them,
And skip ahead. You fidget with the chore -
Weaving a paper-chain to hang before
The two big days. You choose a strip, and lick
One end, and make a loop that doesn't stick.
At last, with perseverance and less spit,
The miracle's done. Pinned up, and fire-lit,
The streaming colours double into shadows;
From wall to wall, cornice to ceiling rose,
Your Christmas birthday, dressed in Christmas cheer!

Gold foil replaces paper-chains that still far-distant year
When you confront your parents, asking why
They had a baby, *then*. Startled, they say
We knew we'd win. How did they bloody know?
Who'd want a black-out baby? Who'd want *you* –
Conceived in bomb-scared dark, for pity's sake,
An ounce of rationed sugar, a mistake
Clammily parcelled in your mother's fear
Till that ill-starred December, '44?
You've seen the cities' hammered stumps and stains.
You've seen the bodies, trashed like last year's paper-chains.

The post-war victory-dawn, more short than sweet,
Dims with the grown-ups' tiredness and defeat:
They tell the same old tales; you roll your eyes…
But now you can't un-link the memories
Of memories they threaded into yours,
That war-time couple, tough and glamorous,

Pluckily 'smiling through' their spoiling future.
We put your basket in the air-raid shelter,
They told you. Snow fell hard. The London sky flashed warm.
Under the earth you slept and dreamt no harm.
Even the bomb that got the house went smash,
Danced with a wardrobe, choked on frocks and suits of ash.
Baby, you're lucky! And you're still alive!

Then raise a sparkling glass, now that you're sixty-five,
To the good love that made you. Weaving wish
To woe in poetry-chains is babyish.
Your first two subterranean weeks prepare you
For the big black-out, so don't let it scare you.
And don't waste day-light asking Was I wanted?
You'll soon be with the dead and unaccounted,
What does it matter? They can't tell you now.
All life is accidental, any how.
And there are soldier-dads this Christmas-time,
Not coming home. For these, too, sip your birthday wine.

Part Three: De Chirico's Threads:
a verse-drama with soundscape

Characters

GIORGIO DE CHIRICO, *Italian painter*, 1888-1978. De Chirico's early work was considered a major contribution to the Surrealist movement, though de Chirico referred to himself as a Metaphysical painter, never a Surrealist. He rebelled against his early style, and re-invented himself in the 1920s and '30s as a neo-Classicist.

ALBERTO SAVINIO, musician, writer, artist, Georgio's younger brother, originally Andrea de Chirico. I have used his pseudonym throughout the play.

ADELE DE CHIRICO, Giorgio's younger sister who died at the age of six.

ARIADNE, the mythological Cretan princess helped Theseus kill the Minotaur and then to escape the tunnels of the labyrinth by means of a guideline of thread. She and Theseus escaped to the island of Naxos, whereupon Theseus abandoned her while she slept. In some versions of the legend, she was later 'rescued' by the god Dionysus. Classical statues of the abandoned princess are depicted in much of de Chirico's early work. In the play, Ariadne is everywoman, and embodies his various muses.

MAMA, Gemma de Chirico neé Cervetto, Giorgio's mother.

PAPA, Evaristo de Chirico, Giorgio's father, a railway engineer and poly-math. The family, though Italian, was based in Greece during Giorgio's childhood and youth, and Evaristo was in charge of developing a new railway system which helped in the transport of armaments to the Greeks in their war with Turkey. Papa has died just before the start of the play, so the Papa we hear speaking is only as Giorgio imagines or remembers him.

LE POÈTE ASSASSINÉ, This character represents the Surrealist writer and artist, Guillaume Apollinaire, and is named after the protagonist one of Apollinaire's stories. Known as 'Le Poète' in the text, he symbolises artistic innovation. Apollinaire died in 1918.

CHANGE-IT, a newspaper editor.

CHANCE-IT, a columnist.

ANONYMOUS POET, a loser.

BRETON, the surrealist artist, poet and activist, Andre Breton.

CARRÀ, Carlo Carra, painter, friend and rival of de Chirico.

EXPERT, art-buyer and critic, always in on the latest trends.

FORGERS

MINOTAUR, the offspring of Pasiphae, wife of King Minos, and a bull. King Minos kept the monster confined in a labyrinth constructed by Daedalus.

SCENE ONE

(1905. GIORGIO, 16, and ALBERTO, 13, watch a train cross a bridge at the end of their street in the Thessalonikan town, Volos.)

(Steam train in the distance, sounding whistle.)

GIORGIO:
Papa, is that you, Papa?
Listen, the minotaur train, sobbing itself to madness
Over and over the arches, the shuddering bridges.
And the going gets faster and darker.
When I was a child, I thought he'd built every train
And every train would be bringing him home again.
Is that his whistle? Is that his steam? And why
Do the clouds get smaller and smaller as the funnel rushes forwards?
Papa, is that you?

ALBERTO:
You know he won't come back. You're scared
To say it, but I'm not. Papa's dead!
He beat the Turks! He died with a gold medal!
Now he's a black-faced angel. Or a golden devil!

(Fade up noise of steam train, crescendo, then slow decrescendo.)

GIORGIO and ALBERTO:
Always on time, always on time
By his watch, on the dot of midday,
Sobbing and screeching, a minotaur fire at its heart,
Driving it on, down a line it can never escape.

ALBERTO:
It was his favourite train, the Athens Express.
When I was small, I asked him, "Are you an engine driver?"
He said, "Alberto, I'm the engine and driver.
I am the engineer!"

PAPA (*voice offstage*):
Our lines are iron but supple,
Tempered and true to the topological laws
And the handbook printed by Thessalian Railways:
'Timetables you can trust! Engines that never go bust!'

GIORGIO:
His perspectives flowed in steel, over rivers and under the mountains,
They flowed from the rock he tapped
And he followed them, setting their course like a god of streams.
Once, he reached Argos, brought us the golden fleece.

ALBERTO:
Turklish Delight – and dates
And almonds and bunches of mint – he was on the right track!

GIORGIO:
When he came back, I was scared
He had left a bit of himself at some station or other –
A tribute to Hermes. He always seemed distant. Smaller.

ALBERTO:
But that's how fathers are. I'm not going to be a father!

GIORGIO:
It comes on the dot of mid-day, and we must board it soon,
When all I want is for time to settle, and silence
Return with a row of grey tears
Fading in lavender sky.

ALBERTO:
We'll jump from the shadows, we'll declare war on railways
And fathers and trains on the dot!
Call up your maidenly muse. I'll master the twelve tone scale.
Greece is for minotaurs. Art
Is the line the amazing De Chirico brothers follow!

SCENE TWO

(Fade up ALBERTO'S music: chromatic piano scales. This fragments into single notes that are ADELE'S music. We hear a child's feet running, and a child wordlessly singing.)

ADELE *(calling)*:
Giorgio, Giorgio, take me with you.

GIORGIO:
Little sister! Little ghost.

ADELE:
Follow the thread and you'll see me, Giorgio.

GIORGIO:
Little sister, little lost Adele!
How did you reach me, here
Where childhood ends? What thread did I clutch and pull?

ADELE:
Giorgio, taller than ever, and still
Loopy and lost in your maze!
I was drawn by the same old sadness
Of seeing our furniture wander
Outdoors, the poor drowsy sofas and eloquent, chattering chairs
Under the stars, while the earth wobbles and reels,
And Mama tries to smile, and says prayers.
It's an earthquake, the death of a father.

GIORGIO:
We must move, says Mama.
We must study in Germany, then go home to our country,
Italy, where we belong. The De Chirico graveyard!
I belong here.

ADELE:
You always hated trains, you thought they were monsters.

GIORGIO:
Yes, I liked kites, that rustled faintly and flew
So high they were lost in the sun.

ADELE:

We used to call you 'kite-boy.' Well, now you can try.
Make your own wings, and fly.

GIORGIO:

You had a hoop. It bounded in front of your hand –
I loved the way it danced for you, spinning so fast as it turned
This way and that. Your sky was the ground. And under...

ADELE:

You learnt to draw on the ground.

PAPA (*voice offstage*):

A permanent job on the permanent way
Isn't for your sort. Art?
I've no objection to Art.
It's tradition, not fantasy, boy.
Copy the masters, that's the way.
Copy the lines that have lasted.

ARIADNE:

He took your hand, like this.
And drove it over the clumsy figure you'd drawn.
With your finger in the sand: he made two crosses.

PAPA (voice offstage):

One for the head, one for the body. Proportion's
The key, boy!

ALL TOGETHER:

A cross for the head and a cross for the heart.

GIORGIO:

I saw how a line is muscle as well as bone
How lines could lead along archways of time – mere lines!

ADELE:

Line – what a long thin word.
A line can be long as a life stopped still –
This is mine – wound up in the ball
Of pain I dreamt was a ball of scarlet twine.

GIORGIO:
No, no! Do you suffer it still?

ADELE:
And yours is the line to Athens, and on to Milan, and on.

GIORGIO:
But how do I draw you back?

ADELE:
Rails run away but they stay, the line always leaves you a line.

GIORGIO:
Will you leave me a line, Adele,
For the maze I must thread, for the monster I must master?

ADELE:
My ball of scarlet twine, if you take me with you!

SCENE THREE

(Train approaches with MINOTAUR noises. They blend to café music and we arrive in 1914, the Cafe Kubik, Paris. LE POÈTE ASSASSINÉ is host to a group of artists and poets. He has invited the newly arrived young artists, GIORGIO and ALBERTO DE CHIRICO, to participate.)

CHANCE-IT:
Pardon me, are you by any chance one of the new rising stars?

LE POÈTE:
I am Le Poete Assassiné, otherwise known as Guilliaume Appollinaire, orphan of the sex-storm, champion of the badly loved and ready to bleed for the cause of artistic brutality. I am no rising star. I am the risen sun.

(Applause)

CHANCE IT:
Honoured to meet you, Mr Apollo. I am Mr Chance-It, the well-known columnist and art-critic of the *Daily Dada*. This is my editor, Mr Change-It.

ANONYMOUS POET (*shouting from audience*):
You're in the wrong place – this café is for artists!

LE POÈTE:
That's why they're here. These indispensibles are the mega-mouths of every new movement. They are our vital publicists, at least until another new movement dawns, when they will merely be cysts with no public. Art must blush seen. Sit down, friends, the stars are on their way.

ANONYMOUS POET:
Journalists! Thugs who beat up words. We're poets! We make love to words.

CHANCE-IT (*announcing*):
This week, Poetry is rubber gloves, dreams that money can buy, codology, cabaret and Laocoon.

(Mixed reaction from audience)

CHANGE-IT:
This week, Art paints with scissors, with sacking, with ecstacy.

CHANGE-IT:
Tomorrow's artist will be an avatar of liberated humanity!

(Cheers from audience)

CHANGE-IT:
That was yesterday's, Chance-It. Tomorrow's artist is the alarm-clock on the tiger's mantel-piece. Let me introduce you to Mr. Tick-Tock!

(A clock is wound and begins to tick. The crowd boos and cheers.)

ANONYMOUS POET:
Where are the wonder-twins you promised us?

LE POÈTE:
 Dark engine, hiding your ruby fire, your brow

Dripping the snows of dead summer, the sweat of dreams,
Your steam is seeping through Paris. Do you bring salvation
Or sal volatile? A mutilation, a muse, or a two-headed monster?

ANONYMOUS POET:
That's what we all want to know!

CHANCE-IT:
Georgio was eating pizza while reading Nietzsche in the Piazza.

MAMA (voice offstage):
Take care – you'll have indigestion.
Never mix lunch with a philosophical question!

CHANGE-IT:
The Dithyrambs of Dionysus! Nice!

CHANCE-IT:
Nice – though not very spicy, not very up-to-the minute, wouldn't you
say, Mr Tick-Tock?

(Audience catcalls)

CHANGE-IT:
He traces his ancestry back to the Argonaut Jason.

LE POÈTE:
Has mama lost her astrolabe at the railroad station?

*(Crowd boos and heckles. There is a shot. Clock stops. Pandemonium. Distant
singing & marching & sounds of war.)*

LE POÈTE:
Boum boum bongo boum
The dithyrambs are dumb as doom.
The only echo's Doric.
Come on boys, get choric.
Italy boum. Liberty boum. Beat the dumb *tamburo* boum
The drum bleeds, we all bleed. Bingo!

(Fade up. GIORGIO and ALBERTO, arguing.)

GIORGIO:
  War's for those the muse has never sung to!
  There are no nerves any more at the ends of their fingers,
  They can't be born, they can't breathe, till they see bloody bone
  Flying in splinters. War's the Minotaur's mother.

ALBERTO:
  Brother, War is the great Because in the great outdoors.
  Let's march – and come back heroes!

GIORGIO:
  I have no cause but the sadness of afternoon,
  the lilac enigma of night-fall.

MAMA (voice offstage):
  Fly, my delicate children, my dioscuri.
  Practise your scales, Alberto, the world's not black and white.
  Split in a thousand colours! Take flight!

LE POÈTE (*to audience*):
  I've no mama with wilting apron strings
  Who swears her son's got genius, and wings.
  I live in the world, I'm loyal to no country,
  Who am I, then? I am the homeless century –
  That pustular puzzled punitive adolescent.
  Find me a gun. I'll brawl like any peasant,
  Fire canon-balls as big as your dreams and swallow
  Swords of all sizes. I am the god, Apollo.
  But I'm not afraid to put on mortal form
  And stride in sweating khaki into the storm.
  I shall bring back such a prize. Not rapture but rupture.
  The brutal beautiful bloodily wounded bull, the Art of the Future.

SCENE FOUR

(Enigmatic music, perhaps solo lute or mandolin. ADELE'S song. Her foot-steps, passing.)

GIORGIO:

The whole world, down to the marble buildings and fountains
Seemed to me convalescent. The autumn sun,
Cold and unloving, lit the statue
And the church façade[1]
I was seeing it all for the first time – the zeugma
Of dreams, the dreaming yoke. It was an enigma.

SCENE FIVE

(Noises of train, interior. ARIADNE chats up GIORGIO.)

ARIADNE:

I've been watching you sketch. You're good. Where are you going?

GIORGIO:

Nowhere. Back to the Front, where everything's
Back to front, when all I want
Is to stand in some ancient square
In a certain light, and paint till the farthest column
Is tinier than a chessman.

ARIADNE:

Is it me? It looks like me.

GIORGIO:

No. My sketch-book's full of such faces. All dream faces. But, maybe…

ARIADNE:

I could stand still for you, I could become a line –
The finest line you could draw! I could recline…

(We hear ADELE'S music, far away.)

---

1. fragment of a poem by De Chirico.

GIORGIO:

    I see you in white, asleep on a vault made of cruel white marble.

ARIADNE:

    Dying. Voluptuous. Made of the fine lines drawn
    Between death and men, like every woman. Bored,
    Probably, after a while. Hey, but it would amuse me
    To be a guy's muse for a bit. I think it would amuse me.

GIORGIO:

    I remember my sister's small coffin.
    I understood nothing then.
    Papa said death is a secret
    That must be kept from the children
    Like the secrets between man and woman.

ARIADNE:

    By the way, Ariadne's the name.

SCENE SIX

(Faint bar-music. We're in a cheap hotel room. ARIADNE and GIORGIO in bed, post-coitus. Their interlocked speech is in the form of a canzone.)

ARIADNE:

    Giorgio, one day I'll teach you
    About power, about sorrow.
    One day I'll beat you.
    Did your father ever beat you?

GIORGIO:

    Why don't you ask me about the things I know?
    Why do you want to tease me?

ARIADNE:

    It's fun to tease you
    Open and shut. At what age did your mother wean you?

GIORGIO:

    You know she never weaned me, I suck her still.

ARIADNE:

Is she a cow, is she a still?

GIORGIO:

Like you, she's a sea of moonlight. Does that please you?

ARIADNE:

Your mother has made a cross
For her widow back. I'm cross.

GIORGIO:

Don't laugh, then, if you're cross.

ARIADNE:

I shall do what men do to woman – I shall leave you.

GIORGIO:

Railways are dangerous for a girl to cross
And you know what you get when two lines cross? –
A riddling sphinx with a bagful of sorrow –
The sort of creature you wouldn't like to cross.

ARIADNE:

The Sphinx will wink and say "Cross
While the going's good, darling, no-one will know."
I was at school with the Sphinx, didn't you know?

GIORGIO:

At school I learnt to sketch shadow, criss-cross, criss-cross.
When the noon sun shines on the tower and binds me still
To the colonnades, my charcoal buzzes, till…

ARIADNE:

You see death. You tremble still
As his black gown swishes across
The room where you sit.

GIORGIO (*with sketchbook*):

I want to draw you. Lie still,

I want to draw you in my sweet new style,
Under the sheet!

ARIADNE (*yawning*):
A girl has a lot to teach you.
Oh, why do you always make desire lie still
Like a nature morte, like one of those so-called Still
Lifes? Life stilled is a corpse. You don't need sorrow
It's rigor mortis, sorrow
In a body that's ravenous, still.

GIORGIO:
Your body tells me things I already know.

ARIADNE:
It tells you things you don't even want to know.

(ADELE'S music, very faint.)

GIORGIO:
Sometimes I think I know
More than the Minotaur. To distil
The enigma we must peel away all we know.

ARIADNE:
Touch me, Minotaur!

GIORGIO:
    No!

ARIADNE:
Give me your pen, touch me here, and draw a cross.
See. It's all true.
You dreamed up a world with no
Sex or death, the things your father knew.
Things market-women know.

GIORGIO:
And what did your father teach *you*?

ARIADNE:

He said women were good for one thing, and he didn't need to
teach me.

GIORGIO:

Mine tested me with questions. If I didn't know
The answers, he pretended a terrible sorrow.
It was never the least bit useful to him, sorrow.

ARIADNE:

But his son soon learned the art of bee-ootiful sorrow.

(ADELE'S music intensifies and we hear her song.)

GIORGIO:

When we passed the sorrowful coffin, Nurse screamed No!
I clung to the railings, I whispered Sorella, Sorella.
Nurse dragged me away.

ARIADNE:

You were singing *Dove Sono.*

GIORGIO:

And now we've met, and the train stands perfectly still.

ARIADNE:

You're playing statues with your deserter's sorrow.

(The song fades slowly as GIORGIO speaks.)

GIORGIO:

I knew she lay in a white box, in deep sorrow.
And would never again step across
The line between life and death. Suppose I were to cross
The Somme, would you spare me a pinch of salty sorrow?

ARIADNE:

I would say die just enough for death to teach you
The love of life. You need this war to free you.

GIORGIO:
Fall asleep again, so I can dream you.

ARIADNE:
You're nailed to the square, to death's double-cross.

GIORGIO:
I'm still as the gleaming railway line is still –
A perpetuum mobile.

ARIADNE & GIORGIO (*together*):
You will leave me, I know
And we'll echo like footsteps through each other's sorrow.

SCENE SEVEN

(*1917. The Villa Seminario, Ferrara a military convalescent home in which GIORGIO and CARLO CARRÀ are patients. Sound of echoey footsteps, bloodcurdling cries.*)

GIORGIO (*painting as we hear ADELE'S song, faintly*):
The great white canon has fired at the crack of noon.
Apollo himself has come to a high halt
In the middle of the sky,
And the statue, deep in the study of her shadow,
Enters eternal happiness.[2]

CARRÀ (*at the next easel, his voice over-lapping sometimes with GIORGIO'S*):
The shadow washes the murals from my soul.
And the whole banal world is transformed.
The autumn afternoon has arrived
With its clear air and lonely, cloudless skies.[3]

GIORGIO:
Those are my whispers and signs.
Must you always be here at my side, Carlo Carra,
Dipping your brush in my colours?

2. Based on De Chirico's own description, quoted in Magdalena Holzhey, *Giorgio de Chirico: The Modern Myth*, Taschen, Germany, 2005.
3. Ibid.

CHANCE-IT:

    Scandal – our favourite brouhaha!
    Tell us about your quarrel!

GIORGIO:

    It was here in Ferrara, here
    Where we rest and recover. I had the doctor's permission
    To paint. He knew it would cleanse me
    And flush the war-acids out of my brain.
    The enigma came back to me here, and the lines
    Ran like white light. Then this parrot,
    Peeked in at me, and discovered some parrot-passion
    For tubes of paint. He squeezed himself into my glory.

CHANGE-IT:

    Nothing much new in that story!

CARRÀ:

    It was inspiration. Nobody owns inspiration!

DE CHIRICO:

    He was inspired to wave cash
    In Milan, he was inspired
    To mount a so-called-revolutionary exhibition.

SCENE EIGHT

(Footsteps, echoing as in an art gallery.)

EXPERT:

    Ladies and Gentlemen welcome to the new dawn —-
    The Dawn of the Metaphysical!

DE CHIRICO:

    The Daub of the Mega-Delusional –
    Not one of my works is displayed.

CARRÀ:

    The gallery doesn't fancy another arcade!

GIORGIO:

    I built that city. I lived there and I named it
    You stole it and shamed it.

SCENE NINE

(The convalescent home.)

CARRÀ *(to CHANCE-IT)*:

    Allow me to show you my latest:
    The Metaphysical Muse, inspired by a dream I had.
    I chose the simplest subject – an anatomical dummy.
    A cross for the face, crosses for eyes, dead simple
    And rather stunning!

GIORGIO:

    Fetch the police chief. Hang the muse-thief!
    No-one would ever imagine this work was mine.
    The manner's banal, the essential signature
    Invisible.

CARRÀ:

    Who cares what name is scrawled in an unlit corner?

GIORGIO:

    I am speaking not of a name. The style lights every corner! My style
    IS the future!

LE POÈTE *(off)*:

    Let me in, Future!

CHANCE-IT:

    A new patient's arrived, all bandage and stubble.
    He looks like the future of trouble.

LE POÈTE:

    I'm Art baptised by Battle – who are you?

GIORGIO:

    My poet, my soul, my Apollo! You're wounded!

LE POÈTE:
 I opened my shirt and said take me, Death.
 But a Russian girl with flowers on her breath
 Took me instead. He is risen, as the evangelist saith.

GIORGIO:
 But you're wounded, you're bleeding, you're faint.

LE POÈTE:
 It's only red paint. I'm a walking exhibition.

CARRÀ:
 Here, Monsieur, I'm Carlo, Carlo Carrà, the Oracle of the Enigma, the
 Founder of Metaphysical Painting, sir, available at little or no notice for
 gallery-openings, garden fetes, swimming parties, balls, banquets, polit-
 ical parades, funerals and quickie celebrity interviews.

LE POÈTE (to CARRÀ):
 This is the only oracle of the enigma! Though I'm Apollo
 I'm not too proud to play prophet, to cry his name from
   the shadows.
 The avatar of the Minotaur! De Chirico!

GIORGIO:
 And tell this imposter to fade up his own *impostura*.

 (A clock starts quietly ticking.)

GIORGIO:
 When Papa first went abroad I learnt about time,
 I was a clock of desire, a torn calendar.
 I ticked off days till the day before the day
 I'd be able to say, 'Hooray!
 Papa's coming tomorrow.' By the time tomorrow came,
 My joy would already be gone. I'd wait for nightfall. A shadow.

CHANCE-IT:
 You must have been born a Surrealist.

GIORGIO:
 I'm not any kind of an Ist!

CHANCE-IT:
    You are. You're the first!

LE POÈTE (*to* GIORGIO):
    Locked in the labyrinth, look at it.
    Locked in the language you made for it.
    Locked in the clock, locked in the fluted column,
    Locked in the lust of the gallery,
    Locked in the glitz of publicity,
    Locked in the legend. Leg it
    To Rome. I'll find you a buyer
    To feed you a little bread and a little fire.

GIORGIO:
    To Rome! And will I meet the Minotaur?

SCENE TEN

(An attic flat in Rome. Distant piano scales, as ALBERTO practises for a recital.)

ALBERTO (*stops playing*):
    I need the shirt today.

GIORGIO:
    I need the shirt today.

ALBERTO:
    I have to play.

GIORGIO:
    Play nude.

ALBERTO:
    Not here. No way.

GIORGIO:
    Now who's the prude?

ALBERTO:
    You don't need to get dressed.

GIORGIO:
    I'm receiving a guest.

ALBERTO:
    Your heart's desire?

GIORGIO:
    Not her! A buyer.

ALBERTO:
    Bro, you're a liar.

GIORGIO:
    The great André!

ALBERTO:
    André Breton? OK.

GIORGIO:
    But you have got to play.

ALBERTO:
    But you've got to be dressed.

GIORGIO:
    He'll still be impressed.

ALBERTO:
    At least cover your chest.

GIORGO:
    What do you suggest?

ALBERTO (*yelling*):
    Ma, got a vest?
    Giorgio's ill.
    Bit of a chill.

GIORGIO:
    Good luck with the concert.

ALBERTO:
　　Good luck with the corsets.

GIORGIO:
　　Will he think it's a sign of vice?

ALBERTO:
　　Yes — it will raise your price.

(ALBERTO leaves and BRETON bustles into the room.)

BRETON:
　　Perdono, Cameriera. I seek an audience with the artist.

GIORGIO:
　　You already have that honour, *camerata*.

BRETON:
　　Though honour is a bourgeois concept, trite
　　As aspidistras, still, it's only right
　　To honestly admit it when one's honoured.
　　Youth shows the way and steers our Ship Surreal.
　　I kiss your hand, *pittora*. No, I'll kneel.

GIORGIO:
　　Please don't, Monsieur Breton. You'll get paint on your suit.
　　You wish to purchase a painting, I believe.

BRETON:
　　You believe! Dear Signor de Chirico, I believe! I believe in your
　　absolute surreality, your surrealist absolutism and your revolutionary
　　anti-shirtism!

GIORGIO:
　　Forgive my immodest appearance. My brother's got the shirt.

BRETON:
　　Nothing's immodest and everything's appearance.
　　Show me your art, Apparently Shirtless One!

GIORGIO:
　　This is my latest self-portrait.
　　I hope you're not disappointed.

BRETON:

    Prometheus Unbound! Schizophrenology Undone!
    Signor, an article is born!

GIORGIO:

    An article? I hoped you might say 'an artist!'

BRETON:

    I always recognise art, Sir,
    By the way it suggests an article. Something like this:

    'A marble bust in profile
    Scrutinises, from the left of the canvas,
    The fleshed and living face which turns away
    Towards us, frowning, pleading: can you see me?
               Young, troubled, propping
    A staged pensiveness on an elegant fist,
    The painter seems not to realise how he's stared at
    By Professor Marble-Head.
    He's a burnished teenaged prince in the blaze of his mind,
    Blind to the marble judgement
    Of the ever diminishing dead!
               Already, a few white hairs, resembling brush-hairs,
    Tell us time's lips have touched
    The bull-brown coif. He broods
    Like a student at a Viva,
    Like a chess-player, deep in the future
    Which is already past.
    What is his defence –
    Only his genius!
          And what does our Marble-Head mutter?
    "Are you certain, boy? What do you mean by true?
    Watch your innocence, dreamer!"
    The face is almost alive with a father's spite.
    He can't forgive the new.
    Why? Because he dreams, too.
    Dead youth is the swamp that rules him, every night he drowns
    In the tangled midnight embrace, the desperate sputter
    Of thin ejaculate.
             Observer, note.
    In the hoop of the old man's shoulder,
    Round and shy as the sallow heel of Achilles

An apple blooms. It repeats
In exact tonality the irrepressible blush
That troubles the young man's cheek.
    These two are truly doubles.'

GIORGIO:

A subtle analysis. Yes, I painted my future
In some vain wish to avert it.
And found I had opened an ancient, questioning eye
In a dream of deathly white – a living eye!

(ADELE'S song, faintly)

BRETON:

Between you and me, I'd rather he'd stayed dead.
He'd surely pick bones with me, old Marble-Head.
Don't take offence. It's perfectly lovely of course
But a little over-arranged, a little false.
Show me an earlier piece. I especially admire
Your manner of mingling arcades and the tall tower
Like the mingling of man and woman in copulation
To give birth to an artichoke or a railway station.

GIORGIO:

That isn't what I paint. I paint the soul
Of sweet virginity, the Aidel Maidel.

BRETON:

Oh sure. But lift her gown and there's a hole!

(Singing turns into a child's cries, fading)

GIORGIO *(to himself)*:

The ball of scarlet twine, the ball of pain
That she wound and tightened, till kind death loosened it
And freed her from scarlet men
(to BRETON)
This one's called The Child's Brain.

BRETON *(in his writing-an-article voice)*:
Here, the tower dominates the arcades

And the male force is supreme.
That creamy smooth and, yes,
Almost asexual torso
Plump with spaghetti and grappa and meditation
Tantalises us with the longing to touch it.

GIORGIO:
Please, I'd rather you didn't.

BRETON:
Not till it's mine, of course.
Then with a light, soaped finger, once a year
I shall permit myself to masturbate
As I stroke the closed eyes, the fine black dragon-flies
Of the moustache. I shall touch the shy white pecs
And think of

GIORGIO:
A son should not even think of a father's sex.

BRETON:
Certamente! Good sons are blind. They become guide-dogs.

GIORGIO:
It's a work of imagination, Monsieur Breton.

BRETON:
OK. Three grand for your grand imaginings.

GIORGIO:
Don't touch it, yet. All right, it's yours, but gently.
Do what you like but don't let father see.

BRETON:
I'll write a book. Fame's faithless, but print sticks.
I'll make them snap and slaver, the starved critics,
I'll blast your name abroad, till the news breaks
Of the swamp we walk on – dreams, women, sex.

GIORGIO (*upset*):
How can I follow the thread
If it leads to mud? Is he the Minotaur?

BRETON (*leaving*):

You are the Minotaur, Maestro,
You are a telephone line to the Unconscious.
Forget technique. You're a child. Study only atmospheres.

(*Door slams*)

GIORGIO:

Where's the way out? Where's the thread?
Hurry, Adele, show me the way to the white
Chamber, where my enigma
Sings of fleshless things in wine-clear light.

SCENE ELEVEN

(*Cacophony of voices above which MAMA & PAPA converse in about the painting GIORGIO has just sold.*)

MAMA:

It's quite true to life.

PAPA:

Be silent, wife.
I've never been fat.

MAMA:

He saw you like that.

PAPA:

I was built like a train.

MAMA:

But in his child's brain...

PAPA:

He's not a child.
I am defiled.
He's made me blind.

MAMA:
  He means that behind
  Your lids is light.

PAPA:
  Or murderous night.

MAMA:
  I think you look peachy.

PAPA:
  What's more, I told him I'd banned the works of Nietzsche.
  (raising his voice)
  No one in my house is allowed to ride a bicycle, mention the word childbirth or eat a banana without a knife and fork. Do you understand?

SCENE TWELVE

(Art gallery. Echoey footsteps.)

EXPERT:
  Not at all the show I expected. Not one De Chirico.

GIORGIO:
  Everything here, sir, is a De Chirico.

EXPERT:
  Indeed! And you've nothing to tempt an unreconstructed Modernist?

GIORGIO:
  Nothing. This is my latest work. Try and improve your taste!

EXPERT:
  Improve your own, Pittora. You were an artist. Remember?

(Expert's footsteps, as he leaves. Click of high heels approaching.)

ARIADNE:

I loved your enigmas, too. You painted a lovely enigma!

GIORGIO:

Once, when I was boy. But I'm not him.
He was a child. Pictor Optimus sum!

SCENE THIRTEEN

(Baroque music distantly. We're in an art gallery. GIORGIO is copying Titian's Sacred and Profane Love. *We hear LE POÈTE'S footsteps approaching.)*

GIORGIO:

"How art thou lost, how on a sudden lost."

LE POÈTE:

Giorgio, is it you?

GIORGIO:

"Defaced, deflowered, and now to death devote?"[4]

LE POÈTE:

My sweet surrealist, tell me it's a joke.

GIORGIO:

My bright Apollo, back in the light at last.

LE POÈTE:

The surgeon dug out my brain and peered inside.
He found the Mona Lisa. So he buried it again.

GIORGIO:

Can nothing prevent the bleeding?

LE POÈTE:

Only death, Pittore.
Why are you robbing graves and dissecting cadavers?

4. John Milton, *Paradise Lost*, Book 9.

GIORGIO:

   I've dissected the wings of angels, tangled with golden fleece,
   Copied each gown-fold and cloud-furl, crawled on my hands
                                                 and knees,
   Seeking the laurel-crown dropped by the deities.

LE POÈTE:

   The dead man's crown. That line ran out in the trenches.
   We were crowned in dead men's guts. The corpses swelled and split
   Their sides, laughed black and green. Master the palette,
   Become a painter of stenches.

GIORGIO:

   Sit down before you whiten to motionless marble!

LE POÈTE:

   Everything whiten and changes. Didn't we call for change?
   Everything melts into nothing. We called for a war to test us,
   To lure us away from fashion,
   Teach us the matchless style of decomposition.

GIORGIO:

   Even decomposition stinks of high fashion.

LE POÈTE:

   "Dada alone does not smell: it is nothing, nothing, nothing.
   Like your paradise, nothing
   Like your idols, nothing.
   Like your heroes, nothing.
   Like your artists, nothing."[5]

GIORGIO:

   Open your mouth, poor baby, howl the nihilist's nought
   But mind you're not knocked out by a passing thought.

LE POÈTE:

   I miss your mockery. Once you joked in marble.

GIORGIO:

   It was no joke but a prayer to the immortals.

5. Dada manifesto, quoted in Hans Richter, *Dada: Art and Anti-Art*, London,
Thames and Hudson, 1997.

LE POÈTE:

Your muse was blind as an egg but always yolk-ful!

GIORGIO:

Blind to the brimming eye, the lustrous curl!

LE POÈTE:

Dead eyes turn white as eggshell. How much do you earn?

GIORGIO:

Nothing but shame and scorn.

LE POÈTE:

The public is right, for once.

GIORGIO:

"Now whenas sacred light began to dawn
In Eden on the humid flowers that breathed
Their morning incense when all things that breathe
From th'Earth's great alter sent up silent praise
To the Creator and his nostrils fill
With grateful smell, forth came the human pair..."[6]

LE POÈTE:

Unless I scent a new irony in the air.
Unless this is fashion, not passion.

GIORGIO:

Poete, it's passion. I'm gazing back at the past
Like a child entranced by a telephone dial:
They speak to me, dear Titian, Raphael,
Leonardo. Sometimes they call me first!

LE POÈTE:

You that futured in style,
Thoroughly neutered!

GIORGIO:

Style! I see my style
In every gallery, a jaundiced grin
With a five o'clock shadow.

6. Ibid, *Paradise Lost*.

LE POÈTE:

Keep your eye on the minotaur, mate.
He's the big yellow sun who glares at you over the gate!

PAPA (voice offstage):

Hold the line taut and straight.
And never let go. Perhaps you'll build kites one day.
A permanent job on the permanent way
Isn't for your sort. Art?
I've no objection to Art.
It's tradition, not fantasy. Copy
The masters, boy, that's the way
To paint lines that fly.

LE POÈTE:

And pictures no-one will buy.

SCENE FOURTEEN

ARIADNE:

Can you afford to insult all these people, darling?

GIORGIO:

They should all be dismembered!
How dare they shrivel me into Mr. November.
And bay – how horribly they bay -
That my only season was May – and it lasted a day!

ARIADNE:

If you painted me again, you'd soon be OK.

GIORGIO:

I have outgrown that marble theatre. I have soared above it. In fact I
suspect at times my painterly technique reaches that of Titian. Of
course the crowd can't see through the eyes of a Titian.

ARIADNE:

Caro, tell me, why am I the only one who appreciates your sweet new
style?

GIORGIO:

Because they're cabbages- and you are a caryatid.

ARIADNE:

How cute. But don't you think it's damned unfair.
The parasites so rich, the host so poor?

GIORGIO:

Has the poet been treating you well? Have you exchanged sweet
Favours, subtle flavours?

ARIADNE:

His subtlety's in some doubt. And he's hardly Croesus.

GIORGIO:

We know the market place wasn't built on Parnassus.

ARIADNE:

Listen. I've got my own muse. She lives in my eyes.
To make myself lovely's an art – not less than yours.
And what she needs is money – not minotaurs.
She looks at me from the mirror.
She loves silks, trinkets, rings.
Her beauty's the line and light of brilliant things:
Brilliant men, too. Though they are increasingly few.

GIORGIO:

I believe I might be growing out of you.

ARIADNE:

But couldn't you make a little copy or two?

GIORGIO:

A copy of you?

ARIADNE:

A copy of you. The early De Chirico.
The one we all loved, the one they wanted to show.
The one who painted my bee-ootiful sorrow...

GIORGIO:

Copy his childish enigmas? Copy his ignorant youthful dreams?
A copyist? Me?

ARIADNE:

You copied the masters. It's what artists do.
Ask some of your students to copy you.
It's simple, and so pedagogical!
The masters learn from the masters, the juniors go to school
With Mr. and Mrs. Metaphysical.
Painters go back to first drafts - it's not a crime.
You'll still be Pictor Optimus — in your spare time

SCENE FIFTEEN

(A studio. We hear a jazzy arrangement of earlier enigmatic music. Sounds of hasty painting.)

CHORUS OF FORGERS:

We're faking him
We're making him
Famous again
Copying the dead man. That's what.
Copying the copies and — why not?
Fame for him
Cash for us
BRAVO FOR PICTOR
OP-TI-MUS!

GIORGIO (*off*):

Forgery! Murder! Monstrosity Carrà
Mirrored in horror.

FORGER:

Delivery daily on the dot! Money-back guarantee, if you can spot
Any difference from the originals -
Own your own stylish De Chirico metaphysicals!

EXPERT:

   The definition of style, gentlemen, is a manner that can be copied
   By those that have neither a style – nor manners.

FORGER:

   Style sells. His name spelt style
   But that was once.
   His latest style's past-tense.

ARIADNE:

   That's right – more white – less red.
   Make the train darker, creeping up like dread!

FORGER:

   Dread sells. His name spelt Dread
   But that was once.
   Today his Dread's past-tense.

ARIADNE:

   More white – the sky needs light.

FORGERS:

   Light sells, but that was once.
   The dunce forgot the public appetite.

GIORGIO (*off*):

   I toiled like Dante and you talked of fashion.
   I had a sacred mission.

EXPERT:

   It's the essence of the essential question
   For the posthumous man.
   The difference between a De Chirico
   And a (*curling fingers here*) 'De Chirico'
   Is academic. But if you can spot the difference
   Get in your research grant applications now!

(Knocking on a door)

GIORGIO:
Papa, is that you, Papa?

EXPERT:
No. So you've still nothing to tempt an unreconstructed Modernist?

GIORGIO:
Not you, again.

BRETON *(voice offstage)*:
It's the Rich Admirer come begging,
Flush at his door with dollars and deadly
Flattery, begging to buy.

EXPERT:
Name your price. How about a private jet,
An expensive pet, a sure-to-win bet?
How about another exhibition.
To convince us philistines that you're the new Titian?

GIORGIO:
Listen! There's an unsold
Canvas, a beauty, one of my favourites but yours
If you can meet the price. Come back tomorrow.

EXPERT:
I don't want a forgery, mind.

GIORGIO:
What exactly do you want to find?

EXPERT:
I want a De Chirico. Painted! By! You!

BRETON *(voice offstage)*:
He worked all night, he painted the perfect tower, the strange
colonnade,

The replicate vision, watched by the Academician.

GIORGIO:
The great white canon has fired the crack of noon,
Apollo himself has come to a high halt
In the middle of the sky,
And the statue, deep in the study of her shadow,
Enters eternal happiness.

(We hear ADELE'S song.)

EXPERT:
Now sign it, sign it! Wait!
We don't want today's date
Spoiling all that good trickster work,
You jerk!

SCENE SEVENTEEN

CHANGE-IT:
Why does Giorgio have a bed that stands six feet off the ground?

CHANCE-IT:
Because he's superior to all other painters?

CHANGE-IT:
Because of the piles of masterpieces underneath it!

CHANCE-IT:
Not!

CHANGE-IT:
He keeps discovering new ones. I did this twenty-five years ago. Want to buy it?

CHANCE-IT:
In fact, he only painted it yesterday.

CHANGE-IT:
Is it a copy? No – it's a re-interpretation.

BOTH:
  Not.

CHANCE-IT:
  What's the stink of the new? That scent's called Déjà Vu.

CHANGE-IT:
  Metaphysical moth-balls! Enigma or dogma?

CHANCE-IT:
  You can't teach an old dogma new tricks.

  (CHANGE-IT howls.)

SCENE EIGHTEEN.

(Funeral march. A graveyard.)

BRETON:
  The talent shrank,
  The fire sank.
  Our Minotaur
  De Chirico,
  Alas, no more.

MAMA:
  My son's a great artist. Why's he in such a small tomb?
  Where are the crowds, the big guns, the beautiful speeches?

BRETON:
  He doesn't need much room.
  We've come to bury his soul.

MAMA:
  What did my poor boy do? It wasn't his fault!

BRETON:
  Don't worry. When you die he'll build you a vault
  Carved into weeping cherubs and all that shlock.
  He's a dinosaur, chip off the old bone-headed block.

ALBERTO:

My brother's not dead! What have you done with him?
We were together just yesterday, planning new work, a trip home.
He said he'd picked up the thread of his inspiration
He'd follow it to Volos, Turin, Rome…
You trend-setters don't rule life and death, though you try.
This date's a lie.

CHANGE-IT AND CHANCE-IT (*triumphant*):
It's the one on his latest painting. De Chirico. 1914.

SCENE NINETEEN

(*Sound of approaching train. Then it fades away. We hear ALBERTO's scales and ADELE'S song.*)

GIORGIO:

Little sister, little ghost.
Do you look at me with disgust?

ADELE:

The disgust isn't mine, it's your own.

GIORGIO:

They damned me for moving, for tapping my own silver track
Into the future.

ADELE:

The line runs on and runs back.
Sometimes it seems to move east and sometimes west,
Depending on how the sun catches it.

GIORGIO:

I stole back my style, because it was mine to steal.
My sight, my truth, after all.

ADELE:

But was it the truth that once,
When the autumn light was clear

And the shadows long in the square,
Shook you with pity and terror?
Were you merely watching the past in a tarnished mirror?

GIORGIO:

How many times can an artist bear that cry –
Your time is gone, your talent's spent, why didn't you die?

ADELE:

Poor Giorgio, poor ghost -
How you tugged at the thread of the past.

ARIADNE (*echoing in his head*):

Impressionism, expressionism, dadaism, vorticism, futurism, surrealism,
constructivism, abstract art, abstract expressionism, cubism, conceptual-
ism, installation, pop art, perfomance art.

GIORGIO:

Guilty of murder, ALL OF YOU.

ARIADNE:

We answer the times. Machinery, markets and war
Scissor the vision.

GIORGIO:

That miserly miniscule vision!
You reduced art to slops.
Character vanished, enigma dissolved
Into brush-strokes, dots and drips.
When I look at you I smell plastic –
Cheap paint, chemical odours.
De Chirico grinds his own colours!

ARIADNE:

Is the business of art to grind paint?

GIORGIO:

You think its business is 'torment?'
I say it's technique.
Tempera, primer and varnish and skill.

ARIADNE:

You speak like that engineer whose lines stand still.

GIORGIO:

You speak with the voice of the dead. Go down with the dead!

(Sounds off of physical attack)

LE POÈTE:

Kill her. Kill Art. It makes no difference. The age is double-dyed.
Appollo is dying. But if you do,
It will be your own suicide.
My broken friend, you are part of it.
Pastiche is the other crime she forgot to mention.
You copied the masters, you copied yourself. Re-invention
Is bound in the same ball of twine, at the heart of it.
Giorgio, true postmodern! Time for a modernist
To join the army of skeletons. Enlist!

(Returning to the present):

GIORGIO:

Something went wrong with the light, so I fixed a new bulb
                                           to the sun.
The enigma screeched like an advertising slogan.
I crippled the horses and statues. The bathing huts were gone,
And the divers had vanished under the blue-green wave.

ADELE:

Time loves what it's lost. Everyone's winter years
Hang like an ill-fitting suit on hungry time.

GIORGIO:

Does art have only one song, does it die after adolescence?
Is it merely the clutter of toys
Untidied, the under-the-bed of little boys?

ADELE:

The ball of twine is long as life, if you trust it.

GIORGIO:

And so I've nothing to fear. The grave's unsealed.

I can play with all my old toys, become a child.
Let's dive, one last time, under the blue-green wave!

ADELE:
But what will you find, now your childish wounds have healed?

ARIADNE:
When artists become the museum, the muses catch the last train.

GIORGIO:
Odysseus will set sail
On the old blue nursery rug, into rocking-chair harbour.
At the customs house he'll pay duty on a roll of wall-paper.

EXPERT:
Dada laughed at the dado – now the dado winks at Dada.

ALBERTO:
The days will dissolve like salt, like a brothers' quarrel.

ARIADNE:
I'll lie like a shell where the waves are slow and long
And Dionysus will hold my white ear to his shadow.

CHANGE-IT (*interrupting*):
And here's some news just in: Monsieur de Chirico
Is nominated by the Academie des Beaux Arts
An Associé Ètranger. He may be a goner
But he still gets the honour. Two cheers for the old conner!

CHANCE-IT:
Time for your comeback, Monsieur!
No need to comb your hair. Swear
If you want. Be rude.
Folk want the wild artist, dude.
They don't like cooked, they want raw!

GIORGIO:
Small-voiced men with microphones in your fat fingers,
Painting and warring and dreaming, the restless Minotaur
Howls for you still, howls for the blood of the new.
Ah, power of youth, of spring! Friends, as we taste its passing
We find our enigma.

(Canzone for all)

GIORGIO:
> In the drawing halls of the academy
> No word was breathed about a minotaur.

MAMA:
> My boys were the best in the academy!

GIORGIO:
> Technical matters constantly occupied me.

ARIADNE:
> Thorns for the brain!

LE POÈTE:
> I pulled out the thorns. *La fenetre s'ouvre comme une orange.*[7]

CHANCE-IT:
> There were not enough windows in the Academy.

GIORGIO:
> I never claimed there was nothing the Masters could teach me.

ARIADNE:
> I taught him plenty! I was his plaster cast.

CHANGE-IT:
> And you were the biggest bust in the whole fancy cast.

ARIADNE:
> Then he abandoned me.

LE POÈTE:
> If you gulp the Mavrudian moon, be careful:
> Oranges fall by the cart-ful.

7. Guillaume Apollinaire, 'Les Fenetres'.

GIORGIO:

At first I was my father's son. Careful.
Chafed by the rules of the academy.
But careful.

CHANGE-IT:

Careful, I think I smell a cowfield
Or something likely to rouse a Minotaur.

LE POÈTE:

Madmen are hopelessly careful.

GIORGIO:

The poet who fights the dragon should be careful
He doesn't start spouting orange
Smoke from his own flared nostrils.

ARIADNE:

Peel me an orange!
Then give me a lift in your long, slow caravan.

CARRÀ:

Shall I accompany you when you are cast
Into the pit, dear madame?

ARIADNE:

Fuck you, plaster cast!

GIORGIO:

I studied the train and the triangle. Runes were cast.
A crystal-ball of greenish sky was cram-ful
Of stars. I married the home-made bone-white cast
To the engine. Oh, such curious shadows were cast
Far beyond the halls of the academy.

CHANGE-IT:

Then the noble philosopher tripped on a wormcast.

ALBERTO:

There are worms in any cast.

GIORGIO:

I befriended a minotaur
Who believed it was I that was the Minotaur.

LE POÈTE:

So countries go to war. And two old friends are recast
As a pair of snarling orange
Hypocrite pussies. How curious orange is,
And death.

GIORGIO:

The cock crowed thrice and the western sky was orange
And terrible. Hooks with glittering flies were cast.
My youth was someone else's, out of range
But everyone wanted me to re-arrange
My toys.

MAMA:

He flew to New York. Gridlocked, gleaming, car-ful.
Momma, he said, an artist must have range
Just like a department-store.

CHANGE-IT:

But the best-selling range
Ran out.

GIORGIO:

I returned to the Academy –
This time it was an elite Academy.

LE POÈTE:

And sensibly they had banned the colour orange.

BRETON:

I wrote a brilliant essay about the Minotaur.

CARRÀ:

I didn't ever think of the Minotaur.

ARIADNE:

I thought of him. Oh silk-horned Minotaur
No woman really fears you! He was a bit deranged,

My husband, always out walking the minotaur
He said. A Minotaur likes an occasional tour.

BRETON:
And is better company than a plaster cast.
You can never go wrong with a pedigree Minotaur.

CARRÀ:
What was he really like, your Minotaur?

GIORGIO:
He was charming and playful,
Slightly arthritic, sometimes pompous but cheerful.

BRETON:
Are you quite sure it was a minotaur,
And not the clockwork bull the academy
Tipped, who tootled, Yoo-hoo, it's only furry-faced me.

GIORGIO:
No-one can label me,
De Chirico, that curious chemical
Which brings on dreams. I was rich, successful, outcast.
Now who becomes the outrageous
Director of the Academy? The Minotaur!

ARIADNE AND GIORGIO (*together*):
Might life not be one vast lie?
Might it be only the shadow of a quick dream?
Might it be only the echo of mysterious
Blows struck against the mountain rocks where no-one
Apparently has seen the other side?[8]

LE POÈTE:
Come and see, children, there's nothing, no side
To the sphere, this terrible orange.

EXPERT:
"How terrible orange is"[9]– now where
Did you hear that before? Perhaps you didn't.

8. De Chirico quoted in Margaret Crossland, *The Enigma of Giorgio de Chirico*, London, Peter Owen, 1999
9. Frank O'Hara 'Why I am not a painter'.

Perhaps it sounds brand new to you. Which doesn't
Mean it is. Quotation lives imperiously
As orphaned memory. We take plagiarism seriously
But is any sentence guiltless of quotation?

GIORGIO:
Art is creation and art is imitation.
Smash the marble, repent.
Sculpt it again and break it again. So my thousand months
    were spent:
Art's whole allegory
And dialectic wove its tale in me!

CHANCE-IT AND CHANGE-IT:
Let the cycle flow. Break out, retreat,
Repeat, invent. Retrieve, revoke. Repeat.

ALL:
Repeat, invent, repeat, invent, repeat, invent.

LE POÈTE AND BRETON:
No, you degenerates! Renew, create!
Renew, create, and never repeat. Repeat! Renew, create and
    never repeat.

CHANGE-IT AND CHANCE-IT:
Repeat, invent, repeat, invent, repeat (etc.)

SCENE TWENTY-ONE

(*The cacophony is silenced by a series of chords played by ALBERTO.
The chords become the chuffing of a train. It slows and stops.*)

GIORGIO:
This is it. The Minotaur's palace. Flat as a factory yard.
Straws flicker in gusts, a child kicks a stone.
And I stand, as always, alone
And, as always afraid.
Some say the minotaur's dead.

He no longer roars but poses for his minute,
Drinking Red Bull on a billboard.
Some say I tamed him years ago. Some say he tamed me.

(MINOTAUR roars)

GIORGIO:

 Wait! Did you hear that? It didn't sound like an imposter.
 I'm not scared. Pictor Optimus sum. Speak, Monster!

MINOTAUR:

Ladies and gentlemen, artists, poets and minor bores, welcome to
 the maze.
You're confused but it's simple. Art is no trick. Art is a lover's gaze.
Always the animal heart must work at art's un-marbling.
Horns push through. But marble is matter, too. It's a little troubling,
Matter. There is no meta. Pure bull, I chew and snooze.
I circle the centre that centres all circles, skulking, cavorting, loose.
Do you think I'm Dionysus? I look the type, shaggy and loud
As if I was rat-arsed and all the crazed Bacchantes were doing me proud.
But no, I'm Apollo, too; Apollo can roar and blaze
And that my friend is the next slippy loop of the minotaur's maze.
I might not rape you: Apollo might. I might be a diagram
Or a baroque fountain. I stink and therefore I am
A chemist of scents, a lacer of threads. Of course it's scary but start
By not making out there are two. There's one strong animal heart.
And don't pretend it's a road. There's no way forward. Progress?
She's the real bull-shitter round here. Run from the rear of that ogress!
 I am as I always was and my pedigree's just like yours.
My horns are my art, self-carved bull-marble. Ladies and briny whores,
Poets and bent-men, geeknesses, Greeknesses, chill.
Call me Dionapollysus: I'm the shitting man's thinking bull.
There is no enigma. De Chirico knows it, and now you're in on the
 joke.
Call me Associate Stranger. The artist. That animal bloke.

(We hear ADELE'S song entwined with slow solo cello music.)

END

Acknowledgements

Acknowledgements are due to the editors of the following: *the TLS, Modern Poetry in Translation, Poetry Review, Poster Poems* (Ed. Billy Mills), the *Guardian's* Ecology Issue (Ed. Carol Ann Duffy, August 2009), the *London Library Magazine, Oxford Poetry.*